blue zoo guides

reptiles and amphibians

by Dee Phillips

TWO-CAN™

MINNETONKA, MINNESOTA

Published in North America in 2006 by Two-Can Publishing
11571 K-Tel Drive, Minnetonka, MN 55343
www.two-canpublishing.com

Library of Congress Cataloging-in Publication Data
Phillips, Dee, 1967–
Reptiles and amphibians / by Dee Phillips.
    p. cm. — (Blue zoo guides)
Summary: "Introduces reptiles and amphibians from around the world,
including information about where they live, what they eat, and how
they grow and survive"—Provided by publisher.
Includes index.
ISBN 1-58728-561-4 (reinforced hardcover)
1. Reptiles—Juvenile literature. 2. Amphibians—Juvenile literature. I. Title. II. Series.
QL644.2.P55 2006
597.9--dc22   2006013268

Picture Credits: Alamy; 90t. OSF; 13, 15, 17, 27, 57, 79

1 2 3 4 5 10 09 08 07 06
Printed in China

Contents

Slime or Scales? 4
Getting to Know Reptiles
  and Amphibians 6

REPTILES
Common Viper 8
Python 10
Boa Constrictor 12
Anaconda 14
Gaboon Viper 16
Black Mamba 18
Coral Snake 20
Corn Snake 22
Emerald Tree Boa 24
Cobra 26
Sea Snakes 28
Rattlesnake 30
Alligator 32
Crocodile 34
Gharial 36
Caiman 38
Gecko 40
Chameleon 42
Iguana 44
Bearded Dragon 46
Frilled Lizard 48
Thorny Devil 50

Thai Water Dragon 52
Blue-Tongued Skink 54
Gila Monster 56
Komodo Dragon 58
Slowworm 60
Tuatara 62
Galapagos Tortoise 64
Sea Turtle 66
Snapping Turtle 68
Terrapin 70
Painted Turtle 72

AMPHIBIANS
Common Frog 74
Treefrog 76
Horned Frog 78
North American
  Bullfrog 80
Poison Dart Frog 82
Common Toad 84
Fire Salamander 86
Japanese Giant
  Salamander 88
Mudpuppy 90
Great Crested Newt 92
Glossary 94
Index 96

Words that appear in **bold** are explained in the glossary.

Slime or Scales?

In some ways **reptiles** and **amphibians** are a lot alike: most of them lay eggs, and all of them are **cold-blooded**. This means that their body temperature goes up and down with the air or water around them. (Your body temperature stays the same, no matter where you are.)

But there are quite a few differences between reptiles and amphibians, if you know what to look for. A reptile's skin is made up of tiny, hard pieces called **scales**. Although some reptiles spend all or part of their time in the water, they have lungs and breathe air. Most lay their eggs on land. Babies look like smaller versions of their parents. Snakes, turtles, lizards, crocodiles, and alligators are all reptiles.

Amphibians have smooth, moist, and sometimes warty skin. They live in or near water, and most of them they lay their eggs in water. Amphibian babies, which are called **larvae** or tadpoles, live and breathe underwater, like fish. As they grow up, their bodies change, and they begin to breathe air. Salamanders, frogs, and toads are all amphibians.

Are you ready to meet some of these scaly and slimy characters? Then turn the page!

Getting to Know Reptiles and Amphibians

The map on this page shows our world.

The blue areas on the map are oceans. The other colors show large areas of land called continents. North America and Africa are continents. Some of the animals you'll meet in this book live on more than one continent. Other animals in this book live on just one continent, or in just one part of a continent.

When you read about an animal in this book, see if you can find the place where they live on the map. Can you find where YOU live?

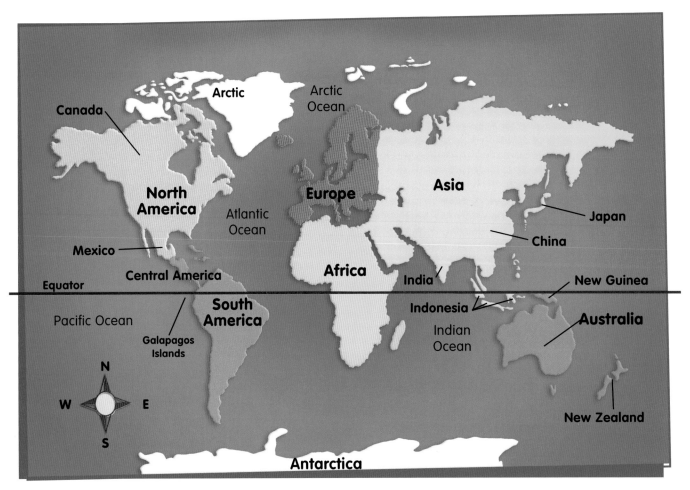

Reptile and Amphibian Habitats

Some animals live in hot places, such as deserts, while others live in forests or in the ocean. The different types of places where animals live are called **habitats**.

Look for these pictures in your book, and they will tell you what kind of habitat each animal lives in.

Deserts – hot, dry, sandy places where it hardly ever rains

Mountains – high, rocky places

Grasslands – dry places covered with grass

Fresh water – lakes, ponds, rivers, **swamps,** or streams

Rain forests – hot, wet forests with very tall trees

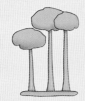

Hardwood forests – forests with trees that lose their leaves in winter

Oceans – huge areas of deep, salty water

Seashores – the shallow salty water and rocky or sandy areas where oceans meet land

Reptile and Amphibian Menus

Some reptiles and amphibians eat only other animals, fish, or bugs and spiders. Others only eat plants. But many reptiles and amphibians eat both animals and plants.

Look for these pictures in your book, and they will tell you what kind of food each animal eats.

Plants

Meat (other animals)

Fish

Bugs or spiders

Common Viper

The common viper is also known as an adder. It lives across most of Europe and northern Asia. It kills its prey by biting the victim with two long, sharp **fangs.**

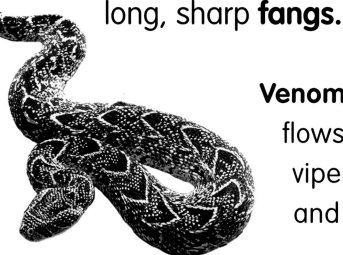

Venom, or poison, flows through the viper's fangs and into its **prey.**

Vipers are often seen sunning themselves on rocks.

A viper eats rats and lizards. It hunts its prey by chasing it or by hiding until an animal comes near.

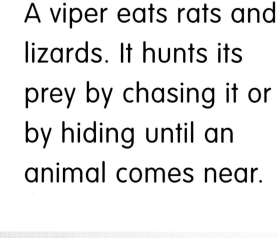

3 ft
0.9 m

6 ft
1.8 m

A female common viper does not lay eggs. She gives birth to 12 to 20 live young at a time.

Vipers can be gray, brown, dark red, or black. Most have a zigzag line running down their back.

Python

Pythons are a group of snakes that are **constrictors.** Constrictors loop their bodies around their prey and squeeze tight to kill it.

Pythons eat animals such as **rodents** and birds. They swallow their prey whole.

The reticulated python (above) is the world's longest snake. Some have grown as long as 33 feet (10 m).

6 ft	12 ft	18 ft	24 ft	30 ft
1.8 m	3.7 m	5.5 m	7.3 m	9.1 m

There are at least 26 kinds of pythons. This is a green tree python.

A python mother lays between 15 and 100 eggs. She keeps the eggs warm with her body until the eggs hatch.

Boa Constrictor

Boa constrictors get their name from the way they wrap their long bodies around their prey. Like pythons, they constrict their bodies (squeeze harder and harder) until the animal stops breathing.

Boa constrictors live in South America and Central America. They hunt at night for small animals such as bats, lizards, birds, rats, and squirrels.

Female boa constrictors give birth to live young.

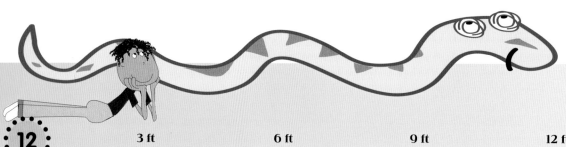

| 3 ft | 6 ft | 9 ft | 12 ft | 15 ft |
| 0.9 m | 1.8 m | 2.7 m | 3.7 m | 4.6 m |

Dark patches of color help boa constrictors to blend in with their surroundings as they hunt for prey.

Anaconda

Anacondas live in South America. They are the heaviest snakes in the world. They can weigh as much as 550 pounds (250 kg). That's as much as three adult men combined!

Anacondas hide from their prey in shallow water. Their eyes and nostrils are on top of their head, so they can see and breathe while their bodies are hidden underwater.

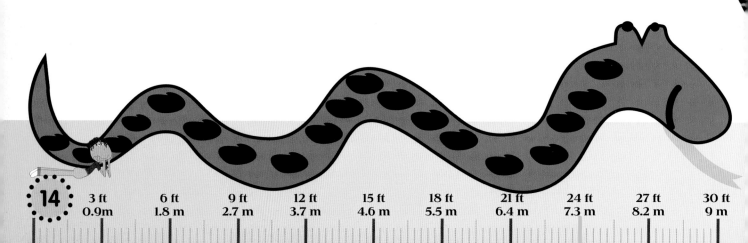

3 ft	6 ft	9 ft	12 ft	15 ft	18 ft	21 ft	24 ft	27 ft	30 ft
0.9m	1.8 m	2.7 m	3.7 m	4.6 m	5.5 m	6.4 m	7.3 m	8.2 m	9 m

Anacondas can catch big animals, such as pigs and deer. They are constrictors.

Anacondas give birth to live baby snakes. The babies can swim and hunt just a few hours after they are born.

Gaboon Viper

The gaboon viper is a kind of **venomous** snake. Its pattern of colorful scales helps it blend into the leaves on the forest floor.

Gaboon vipers have the longest fangs of any venomous snake. The fangs are about as long as your finger!

Gaboon vipers hunt for frogs, birds, and other small creatures.

3 ft
0.9 m

6 ft
1.8 m

Female gaboon vipers give birth to live babies every 2 to 3 years.

They live in forests in Africa.

Like all snakes, gaboon vipers swallow their food whole.

Black Mamba

The black mamba is the most venomous snake in the world. It may also be the fastest.

The black mamba is not actually black. It is usually gray or brown.

It makes its home in a rocky crevice, or crack, or in a hollow tree.

Black mambas come out during the day and feed on birds and **mammals.**

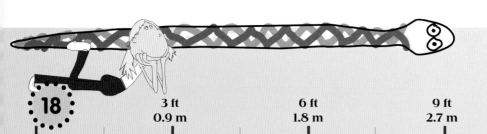

| 3 ft | 6 ft | 9 ft | 12 ft | 15 ft |
| 0.9 m | 1.8 m | 2.7 m | 3.7 m | 4.6 m |

Females lay 12 to 17 eggs in an underground nest.

Black mambas live in eastern and southern Africa.

Coral Snake

These colorful venomous snakes live in warm parts of North and South America. There are about 40 different **species.**

The coral snake's colorful stripes tell **predators** that the snake is **poisonous** and not good to eat.

Coral snakes are small and thin, with a small head and smooth scales.

Coral snakes lay eggs.

3 ft
0.9 m

6 ft
1.8 m

Coral snakes eat other snakes and small lizards. Their venom works quickly to **paralyze** their prey.

These snakes spend their time hidden in the forest. They come out at night to hunt.

Corn Snake

Corn snakes live in the eastern United States. They can be found in trees, on buildings, or on the ground, hiding under logs and rocks.

Corn snakes are constrictors that eat rats and mice.

They taste the air with their tongues to find out if dinner is close by.

They have a Y-shaped tongue.

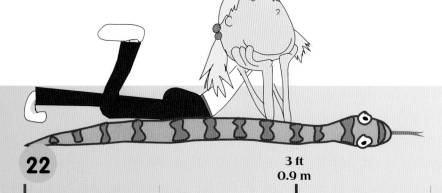

3 ft
0.9 m

6 ft
1.8 m

Snakes have no eyelids. Their eyes are open even when they are asleep.

Female corn snakes lay eggs in piles of leaves. The baby snakes **hatch** about 60 days later.

23

Emerald Tree Boa

Emerald tree boas live in the rain forests of South America. They are constrictors that eat birds, mice, and other small animals.

Its green skin helps the snake hide among the leaves.

Emerald tree boas wrap their bodies around a branch and then reach out with their heads to catch their prey.

3 ft
0.9 m

6 ft
1.8 m

9 ft
2.7 m

12 ft
3.7 m

15 ft
4.6 m

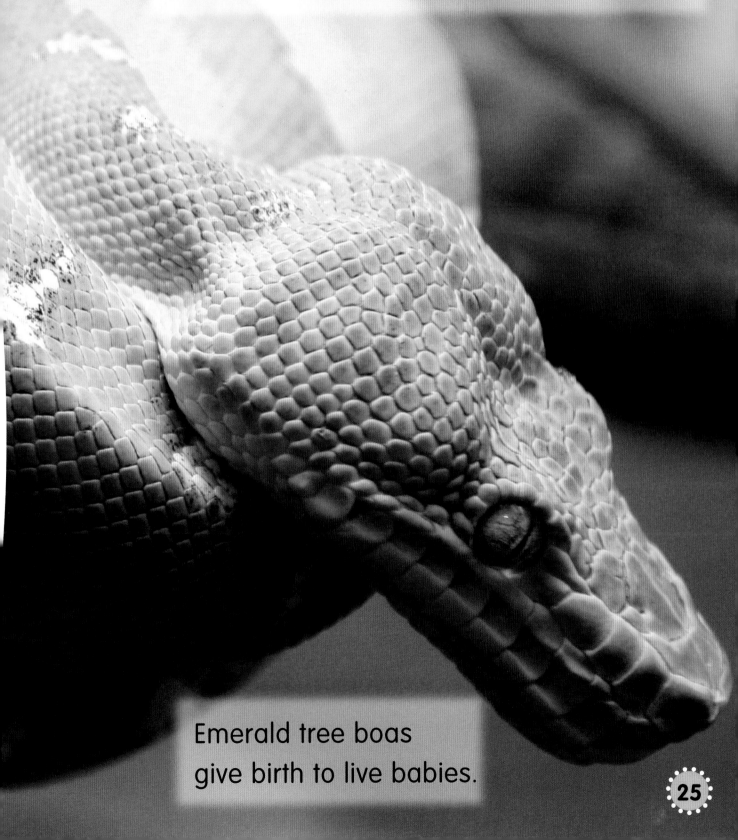

Newborn emerald tree boas are red, yellow, or orange. When they are about one year old, like this one, they start to turn green.

Emerald tree boas give birth to live babies.

Cobra

Cobras are a group of snakes that live in lots of different habitats in southeast Asia and Africa. They are very venomous.

These markings look a little bit like eyes!

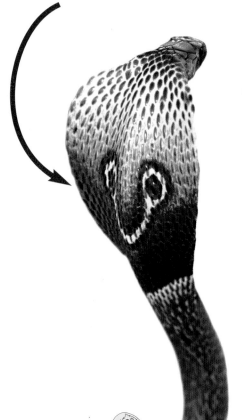

When a cobra meets an enemy, it rears up and spreads a hood of skin just behind its head.

Some kinds of cobras can spit venom from their fangs. The poison can hit prey up to 6 feet (2 m) away.

3 ft	6 ft	9 ft	12 ft	15 ft
0.9 m	1.8 m	2.7 m	3.7 m	4.6 m

Cobras eat rats, birds, lizards, toads, and other snakes.

Indian cobras like this one lay 12 to 20 eggs at a time. The baby snakes hatch after 60 days.

Sea Snakes

Many different species of sea snakes live in warm seas around the world. Like land snakes, sea snakes are reptiles with scaly skin. Sea snakes are highly venomous.

Sea snakes have flat tails that are made for swimming. Their nostrils close tight to keep water out.

Sea snakes must come to the water's surface to breathe air.

Almost all sea snakes give birth to live young. Only the banded sea snake leaves the water to lay eggs.

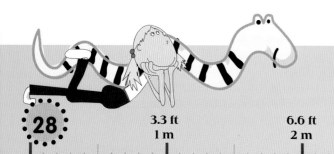

| 3.3 ft | 6.6 ft | 9.8 | 13.1 ft | 16.4 ft |
| 1 m | 2 m | 3 m | 4 m | 5 m |

Sea snakes are usually found in shallow water, where they swim around near the ocean floor. They eat fish and eels.

Rattlesnake

Rattlesnakes are a group of venomous snakes. They catch their prey by biting them with their fangs.

If an enemy comes near, a rattlesnake rattles the end of its tail to say, "Go away"!

Rattlesnakes hunt lizards, birds, rats, and other small animals.

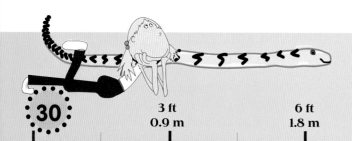

3 ft
0.9 m

6 ft
1.8 m

9 ft
2.7 m

12 ft
3.7 m

This timber rattlesnake lives in the eastern United States. Like all rattlesnakes, it gives birth to live babies.

The rattle is made of hard scales. When shaken, it makes a buzzing sound.

Alligator

Alligators are fierce reptiles that spend a lot of time in lakes, rivers, and swamps. There are two species: the very large American alligator and the smaller Chinese alligator.

An alligator's eyes and **nostrils** are on top of its head so it can see and breathe while hiding underwater.

Alligators hunt for fish, snakes, turtles, lizards, and birds. They gobble up their prey whole.

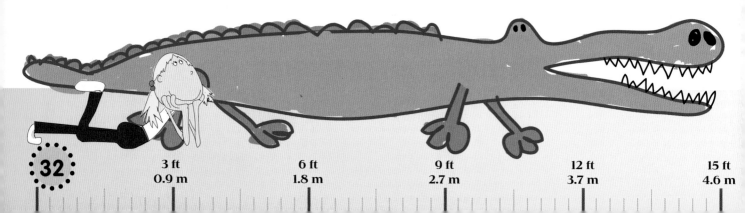

3 ft
0.9 m

6 ft
1.8 m

9 ft
2.7 m

12 ft
3.7 m

15 ft
4.6 m

Webbed feet and a powerful tail make this guy a great swimmer.

Alligator moms may care for their **hatchlings** for up to a year.

Crocodile

Crocodiles are a group of huge reptiles that live in Africa, Australia, and southeast Asia. Most crocs make their homes in fresh water. The saltwater crocodile can live in oceans, too.

Crocodiles will eat anything they can catch, including fish, turtles, and birds.

Female crocodiles lay their eggs in a hole on a sandy riverbank.

Like alligators, crocodiles have very tough skin.

| 3 ft | 6 ft | 9 ft | 12 ft | 15 ft | 18 ft | 21 ft | 24 ft | 27 ft |
| 0.9 m | 1.8 m | 2.7 m | 3.7 m | 4.6 m | 5.5 m | 6.4 m | 7.3 m | 8.2 m |

A crocodile egg is about the same size as two chicken eggs.

Baby crocodiles hide in their mom's mouth if there is any danger.

35

Gharial

Gharials are reptiles that belong to the same animal family as crocodiles. They live in rivers in India and nearby countries.

Gharials have weak legs. When they move on land, they slide along on their bellies!

There are more than 100 needle-sharp teeth in this long, thin snout.

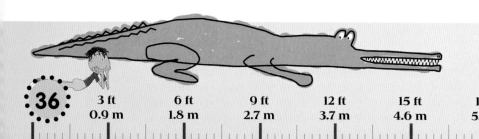

3 ft	6 ft	9 ft	12 ft	15 ft	18 ft	21 ft	24 ft	27 ft
0.9 m	1.8 m	2.7 m	3.7 m	4.6 m	5.5 m	6.4 m	7.3 m	8.2 m

Only the males have
a lump on their snout.

Gharials spend most of their time
in water. Their main food is fish.

Female gharials dig a nest hole
away from the river's edge.
There they lay about 60 eggs.

Caiman

These fierce reptiles are also members of the crocodile family. Caimans live in Central and South America. There are six different species.

Mother caimans use leaves and plants to make a nest for their eggs. The nest may be built to float on the water's surface or to sit on the shore.

Caimans hunt at night for fish, other reptiles, birds, and amphibians.

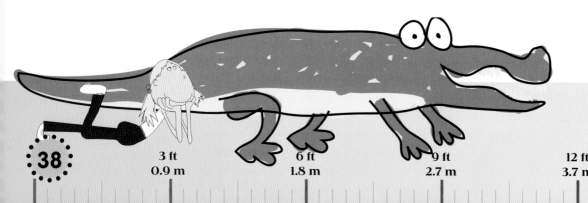

| 3 ft 0.9 m | 6 ft 1.8 m | 9 ft 2.7 m | 12 ft 3.7 m | 15 ft 4.6 m |

Sometimes several caiman mothers share a nest. The females work as a team to guard the nest from predators.

39

Gecko

Geckos live in warm places like rain forests and deserts. They are the only lizards that have a voice. They make a noise that sounds like "gecko." This is how they got their name.

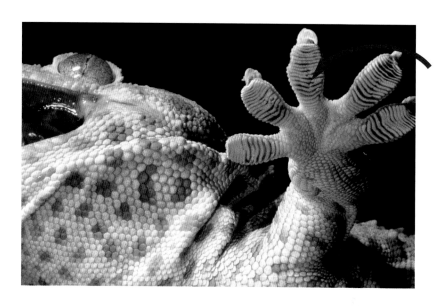

These feet can climb anything —even smooth, slippery glass.

There are about 400 species of gecko. The largest (shown above) is a tokay.

| 4 in | 8 in | 12 in | 16 in | 20 in | 24 in |
| 10 cm | 20 cm | 30 cm | 41 cm | 51 cm | 61 cm |

Geckos hunt at night for insects, but they also eat young birds, eggs, and tiny mammals.

This is a Madagascan day gecko.

Most female geckos lay eggs with soft shells. It takes up to 60 days for the eggs to **hatch**.

Chameleon

Chameleons are lizards with special skin that can change color if they are angry or excited. They also change color to blend in with their surroundings. This is called **camouflage.**

When a chameleon spots dinner, it shoots out its long tongue so fast, you can hardly see it.

It can hold onto branches with its tail.

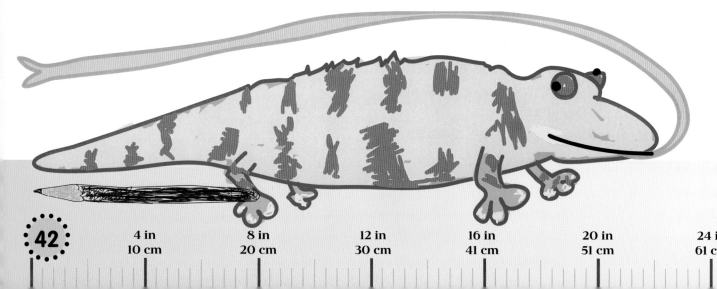

4 in	8 in	12 in	16 in	20 in	24 in
10 cm	20 cm	30 cm	41 cm	51 cm	61 cm

Chameleons can move each of their eyes separately to see in two directions at the same time.

This is a Jackson's chameleon. It lives in eastern Africa and Hawaii.

Iguana

Iguanas are a group of large lizards. Most kinds live in rain forests or deserts. The marine iguana lives by the sea.

Iguanas vary in color from green to brown to yellow.

If attacked, the iguana uses its tail like a whip to fight back.

These powerful legs are great for swimming and for climbing trees.

3 ft
0.9 m

6 ft
1.8 m

A female iguana digs a shallow hole and lays 20 to 70 eggs. Then she covers the eggs with soil and leaves them to hatch on their own.

Iguanas eat mostly plants, insects, worms, and small animals.

Bearded Dragon

The bearded dragon is a kind of lizard. It lives in forests and hot, dry places in Australia. It is named for the spiky scales under its chin.

This spiky skin looks a little like a beard.

If a predator comes near, the dragon puffs up its beard and opens its mouth wide to look scary.

3.3 ft
1 m

6.6 ft
2 m

Bearded dragons often sit on a branch or fence, where they can keep watch over their **territory**.

Bearded dragons eat whatever they can find: bugs, plants, fruit, or small rodents or lizards.

Females lay their eggs in sandy ground. They do not stay to raise the hatchlings.

Frilled Lizard

Frilled lizards live in forests in Australia. They live in trees, but they come down to the ground to search for food.

Frilled lizards eat bugs and other smaller lizards.

When a predator comes close, the frilled lizard opens a big flap of skin behind its head and hisses to make itself seem scary. Then it quickly runs up a tree to escape.

| 8 in | 16 in | 24 in | 32 in | 40 in |
| 20 cm | 41 cm | 61 cm | 81 cm | 101 cm |

The frill folds up flat against the lizard's shoulders.

Female frilled lizards lay about 8 eggs at one time.

Thorny Devil

This strange, spiky lizard is a thorny devil. It lives in the hot deserts of Australia.

The thorny devil tucks its head between its legs when danger is near. Its sharp spikes scare off many hungry predators.

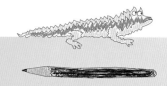

| 8 in | 16 in | 24 in | 32 in | 40 in |
| 20 cm | 41 cm | 61 cm | 81 cm | 101 cm |

These shy lizards can change their skin color to match the sand around them.

Thorny devils eat thousands of ants a day by licking them up, one at a time.

Female thorny devils lay their eggs in underground **burrows**.

Thai Water Dragon

Thai water dragons are large lizards that live in southeast Asia. They live in forests near lakes and streams.

If a predator comes close, this lizard will escape into the water. Its long tail helps the lizard to swim.

Thai water dragons spend time on the ground and in trees.

Long toes and sharp claws are good for climbing.

Females lay eggs in burrows and cover them with dirt and leaves.

Thai water dragons eat small animals, such as other lizards. Sometimes they eat plants.

53

Blue-Tongued Skink

Skinks are a family of smooth, shiny lizards. The blue-tongued skink lives in Australia.

It has a wide head…

a chubby body…

and short legs.

In the daytime, the blue-tongued skink sunbathes and looks for snails, bugs, fruit, flowers, and berries to eat.

Females give birth to 10 to 15 live babies at one time.

3 ft
0.9 m

6 ft
1.8 m

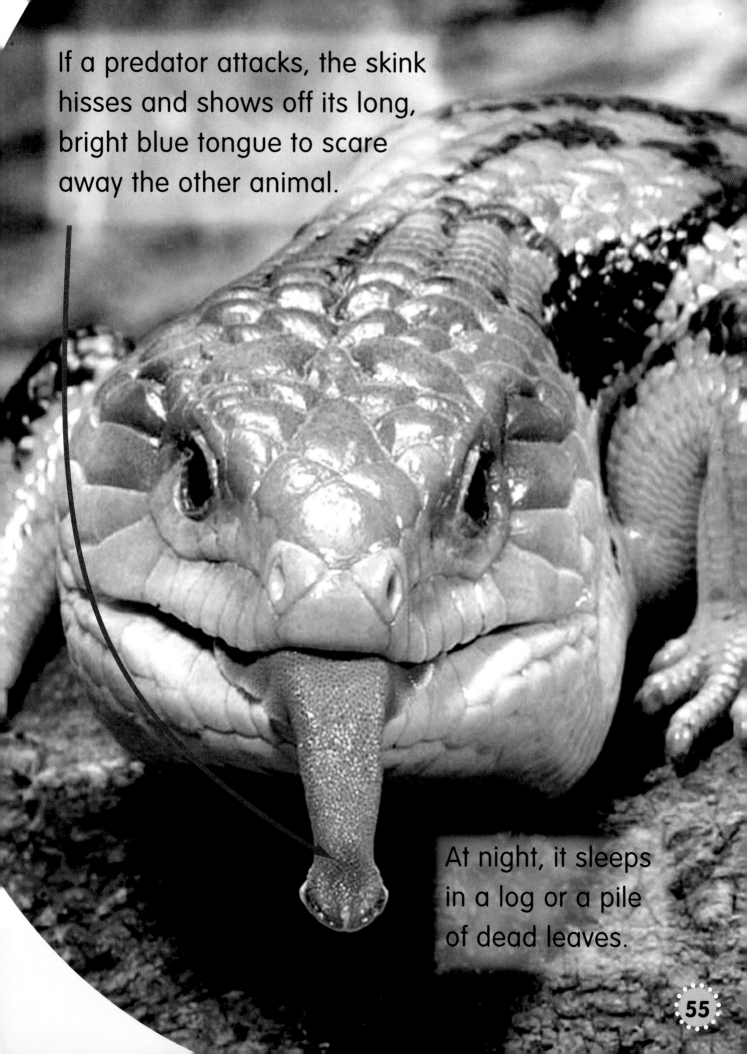

If a predator attacks, the skink hisses and shows off its long, bright blue tongue to scare away the other animal.

At night, it sleeps in a log or a pile of dead leaves.

55

Gila Monster

Gila monsters are big, slow, and venomous lizards. They live in deserts in North America.

They have scaly skin that looks like small beads.

Gila monsters store fat in their tails. When there is no food available, their bodies use this fat for energy.

Gila monsters eat rats, birds, frogs, other lizards, and eggs.

When they bite their prey, venom comes out of their teeth.

| 8 in | 16 in | 24 in | 32 in | 40 in |
| 20 cm | 41 cm | 61 cm | 81 cm | 101 cm |

Baby Gila monsters are
4 inches (10 cm) long when
they hatch from their eggs.

Komodo Dragon

The komodo dragon, also called the komodo monitor, is the biggest lizard in the world. It lives in Indonesia.

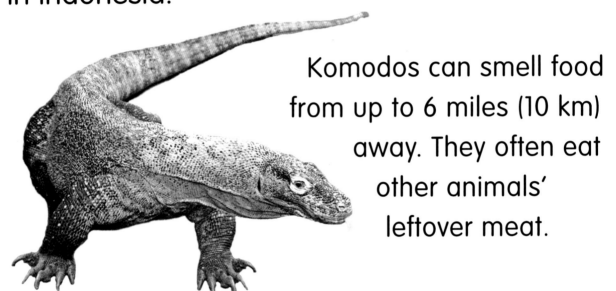

Komodos can smell food from up to 6 miles (10 km) away. They often eat other animals' leftover meat.

The komodo is not venomous. But dangerous germs in its mouth make its bite just as deadly.

Check out this big forked tongue!

3 ft	6 ft	9 ft	12 ft	15 ft
0.9 m	1.8 m	2.7 m	3.7 m	4.6 m

Females dig large
burrows in the sand
and lay up to 30 eggs.

When the babies hatch,
they move into the trees to
stay away from predators.

Slowworm

Slowworms look like snakes, but they are actually lizards with no legs. (Lizards have eyelids, while snakes do not). During winter, slowworms **hibernate** in piles of leaves.

Morning and evening are good times to hunt for insects, worms, and slugs.

Slowworms live in fields and on farmland across Europe and western Asia.

| 8 in | 16 in | 24 in | 32 in | 40 in |
| 20 cm | 41 cm | 61 cm | 81 cm | 101 cm |

If a slowworm is attacked, it can make its own tail break off. This lets the lizard escape. The tail will grow back later.

Female slowworms give birth to live babies.

Tuatara

Tuataras look like lizards, but they are a separate family of reptiles. There are two different species. Both live in New Zealand.

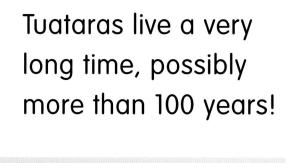

Tuatara eggs develop inside the female's body for up to a year before she lays them. It may be another 14 months before they hatch.

Tuataras live a very long time, possibly more than 100 years!

3 ft
0.9 m

6 ft
1.8 m

They live in burrows and come out mostly at night.

Tuataras eat beetles, crickets, small lizards, and sometimes bird eggs and chicks.

Galapagos Tortoise

Galapagos **tortoises** are the biggest tortoises in the world. They live on the Galapagos Islands, near South America.

They like to munch on plants, grass, and **cactus** plants. They also like to lie in the sun and to relax in muddy puddles.

Like many tortoises and turtles, these giants can pull their head and legs inside their shell.

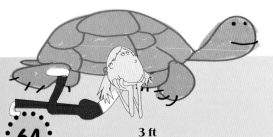

| 3 ft | 6 ft | 9 ft | 12 ft | 15 ft |
| 0.9 m | 1.8 m | 2.7 m | 3.7 m | 4.6 m |

Females dig a nest
in sandy ground.
Their eggs are the
size of tennis balls.

A tortoise is built for life on land,
with short legs and claws. A turtle
has a body made for swimming.

Sea Turtle

Sea turtles are swimming reptiles with hard shells. Many different species live in oceans all around the world.

Sea turtles have smooth shells and long, flat front legs that work like paddles in the water.

Most sea turtles eat meat, but this green turtle eats seaweed.

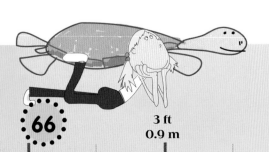

| 3 ft | 6 ft | 9 ft | 12 ft |
| 0.9 m | 1.8 m | 2.7 m | 3.7 m |

Female sea turtles leave the ocean to dig a sandy nest for their eggs.

When the eggs hatch, the baby turtles dash for the water. Hungry predators may be on the lookout!

Snapping Turtle

This fierce reptile lives in lakes, ponds, swamps, and rivers in North America.

The snapping turtle has no teeth. It uses its hard, hooked beak to slice at its prey.

This turtle cannot pull its head into its shell, so it uses its bite for protection.

Females use their back legs to dig a nest. They lay 20 to 30 eggs, then leave them to hatch on their own.

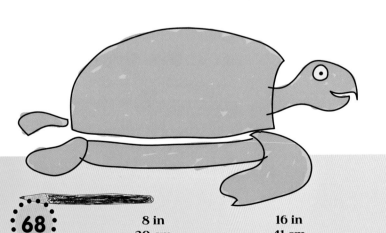

8 in	16 in	24 in	32 in	40 in
20 cm	41 cm	61 cm	81 cm	101 cm

Frogs, toads, snakes, small mammals, and plants are all tasty treats for a snapping turtle.

Snapping turtles often hide in underwater mud and surprise their prey.

Terrapin

Terrapins are small freshwater turtles that live in swamps, lakes, and rivers. They spend much of their lives in the water.

This is a helmeted terrapin. Like all terrapins, it eats meat and catches most of its prey in the water.

Some terrapins can spend the winter underwater, buried in mud.

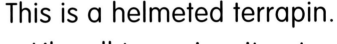

4 in
10 cm
8 in
20 cm
12 in
30 cm
16 in
41 cm
20 in
51 cm

Terrapins, like this diamondback terrapin, lay eggs on land, cover them, and then leave. The hatchlings will take care of themselves.

Terrapins eat fish, snails, insects, and insect larvae.

Painted Turtle

The painted turtle is one of the most common turtles in North America. It spends most of its time in the water, but it may come to shore to sun itself on a rock or a log.

Painted turtles live in ponds, lakes, swamps, and slow-moving rivers.

In the wild, these colorful turtles can live for 5 to 10 years.

| 8 in | 16 in | 24 in | 32 in | 40 in |
| 20 cm | 41 cm | 61 cm | 81 cm | 101 cm |

During very cold weather, northern painted turtles hibernate by burying themselves in mud.

Female painted turtles lay 5 to 10 eggs in a shallow pit that they dig with their hind legs. The eggs hatch on their own in about 10 weeks.

European Common Frog

The European common frog is the most common frog in northern Europe. It lives close to lakes, ponds, rivers, and streams.

Female common frogs lay thousands of eggs at a time. The eggs are called frogspawn. They look like a big clump of jelly in the water.

The baby frogs are called tadpoles. They hatch after about two weeks, if the weather is warm enough.

Frogs use their long, sticky tongues to catch tasty bugs.

These frogs live most of their lives on land. They return to water to **breed.**

Treefrog

Treefrogs live in Australia, New Guinea, Europe, Asia, and North America. There are many different species.

Treefrogs, like this red-eyed treefrog, have sticky pads on their toes that help them climb trees.

These frogs usually come out at night, looking for bugs to eat.

4 in	8 in	12 in	16 in	20 in
10 cm	20 cm	30 cm	41 cm	51 cm

Giant tree frogs are the largest type of treefrog. They can grow to be about 5 inches (12 cm) long.

Treefrog moms lay their eggs in water. One kind, called white's treefrog, lays up to 3,000 at once!

Horned Frog

Horned frogs are large, fat amphibians that live mainly in the rain forests of South America and Asia. There are many different species.

Horned frogs get their name from two pointy flaps of skin over their eyes. The horns are not sharp, but they may look like it to a hungry predator.

Females can lay up to 1,000 eggs. They attach the eggs to water plants to keep them from floating away.

4 in
10 cm

8 in
20 cm

12 in
30 cm

16 in
41 cm

20 in
51 cm

Horned frogs catch lizards, mice, and other frogs by burying themselves in the ground and pouncing as prey passes by.

This is a Chacoan horned frog.

North American Bullfrog

Adult bullfrogs are the largest frogs in North America. They croak loudly at night from their homes in lakes, ponds, and streams.

Bullfrogs eat any animal they can swallow, including other frogs, turtles, birds, fish, and small mammals.

All frogs and toads have back legs built for hopping. But bullfrogs are champion jumpers.

| 4 in | 8 in | 12 in | 16 in | 20 in |
| 10 cm | 20 cm | 30 cm | 41 cm | 51 cm |

These round circles behind the eyes are the frog's eardrums.

Male bullfrogs protect their territory from other frogs by chasing them away, wrestling, and making loud warning calls.

Poison Dart Frog

Poison dart frogs live in rain forests in Central and South America. Some native people use the frogs' poison on arrows for hunting.

Poison dart frogs can be red, blue, or green.

Poison dart frogs lay eggs on land. When the eggs hatch, one of the parents carries the tadpoles on its back to fresh water.

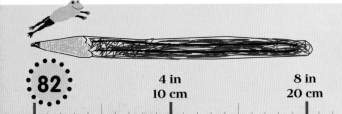

4 in	8 in	12 in	16 in	20 in
10 cm	20 cm	30 cm	41 cm	51 cm

The bright colors of a poison dart frog warn hungry predators that the frog is poisonous.

European Common Toad

The European common toad is one of Europe's most common amphibians. It also lives in parts of Asia and Africa.

These toads spend the day in cool, damp places. They come out mostly at night, looking for bugs and slugs to eat.

Female toads lay long strings of eggs in ponds.

| 4 in | 8 in | 12 in | 16 in | 20 in |
| 10 cm | 20 cm | 30 cm | 41 cm | 51 cm |

Toads and frogs are very close relatives. Toads usually have bumpier skin and spend more time on land than frogs do, but not always.

Fire Salamander

The fire salamander is an amphibian. It lives in forests in Africa, Europe, and western Asia.

Its yellow and black skin tells predators that the salamander has poison on its skin and is bad to eat.

Baby salamanders are called larvae. They are born in fresh water. They swim and breathe underwater, just as fish do.

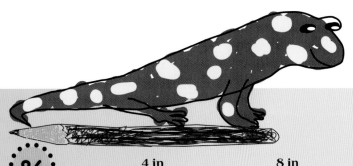

4 in	8 in	12 in	16 in	20 in
10 cm	20 cm	30 cm	41 cm	51 cm

Fire salamanders
eat worms,
slugs, and bugs.

When salamander larvae grow up,
they live on land and breathe air.
Fire salamanders like damp forests.

Japanese Giant Salamander

The Japanese giant salamander is one of the biggest amphibians in the world. It lives in Japan.

These giants do not leave the cold mountain streams and rivers where they live. Adults must come to the surface to breathe air.

Japanese giant salamanders eat many different water animals, including fish, snails, and crabs.

They can go for weeks without eating if there is no food.

3 ft
0.9 m

6 ft
1.8 m

The female lays long strings of up to 500 eggs in a hole dug by her mate.

The male guards the nest until the eggs hatch. Then the larvae swim off on their own.

Mudpuppy

Mudpuppies are a type of salamander. They live in fresh water in southern Canada and parts of the United States.

The mudpuppy has two pairs of legs, each with a four-toed foot.

The mudpuppy's feathery **gills** allow it to breathe underwater, as a fish does. Unlike other salamanders, it does not develop lungs as an adult.

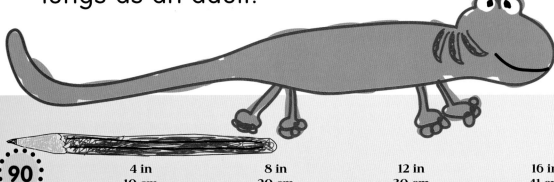

4 in	8 in	12 in	16 in	20 in
10 cm	20 cm	30 cm	41 cm	51 cm

Females dig a nest under a rock or log and guard their eggs until they hatch.

Mudpuppies are brown, gray, or black. They usually have black spots.

Great Crested Newt

Newts are salamanders that return to the water for all or part of the year to breed. Great crested newts live near ponds and lakes in Europe.

In the daytime, these newts hide under logs or stones. At night they hunt for tadpoles, worms, and insect larvae.

Male great crested newts have a jagged crest, or ridge, down their backs.

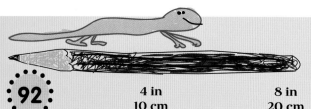

| 4 in 10 cm | 8 in 20 cm | 12 in 30 cm | 16 in 41 cm | 20 in 51 cm |

Female newts lay two to three eggs every day for about five months.

They wrap their eggs in leaves and hide them among water plants.

The larvae live in the water until they grow up. Then they move to dry land.

Glossary

amphibians: animals such as frogs, toads, newts, and salamanders that spend part of their time in water and part on land. Amphibians lay their eggs in water.

breed: to produce eggs or babies with another member of one's species

burrow: a hole or tunnel used for shelter

cactus: a kind of spiky desert plant

camouflage: the ability to blend in with the colors of one's surroundings

cold-blooded: having a body temperature that matches one's surroundings

constrictor: any snake that kills by wrapping its body around its victim and squeezing tight

fangs: long, sharp teeth at the front of the mouth. Snakes' fangs are hollow (like drinking straws) and are used to inject poison into their prey.

frog: any amphibian with smooth skin and long back legs for jumping. Adults have no tail.

gills: a part of the bodies of young amphibians and fish that allows them to breathe underwater

habitat: the place where an animal or plant makes its home, such as a desert or a pond

hatch: to be born by breaking out of an egg

hatchlings: the name for babies (such as baby reptiles) that have just hatched from eggs

hibernate: to spend the winter in a deep sleep

larvae: the name for the young of some animals (such as amphibians) that are in a stage of life between egg and adult. Amphibian larvae are also called tadpoles.

lizard: any reptile with scaly skin, eyelids, and legs

mammals: animals with hair or fur that give birth to live babies and feed them with their own milk

newt: the name for any kind of salamander that returns to water to breed

nostrils: openings in the nose used for breathing and smelling

paralyze: to cause an animal to be unable to move

poisonous: containing poison, which may cause illness or death

predator: an animal that eats other animals

prey: an animal that is food for other animals

reptiles: a group of animals that includes snakes, lizards, tortoises, and turtles. Reptiles are cold-blooded and have scaly skin.

rodents: small, plant-eating mammals such as mice, rats, and squirrels

salamander: any amphibian with a long body and tail and short legs. Salamanders are born in water, but most live on land as adults.

scales: tough, flat pieces of skin that cover the bodies of reptiles

snake: any long, thin reptile with scaly skin and no legs

species: one specific kind of animal, such as the blue-tongued skink. Animals can usually only breed with other animals of the same species.

swamps: areas that are covered in water at least part of the year, with muddy ground that is soft and squishy

territory: an area where an animal lives and feeds. Animals guard their territories to keep other animals from eating the food in the territory or taking the good places to sleep.

toad: any amphibian with rough skin and long back legs for jumping. Adults have no tail.

tortoise: any reptile with a hard shell and legs and feet made for life on land

turtle: any reptile with a hard shell and legs and feet made for life in water

terrapin: any small, freshwater turtle

venom: poison that flows from an animal's mouth parts. Venom is used to paralyze or kill other animals for food.

venomous: able to produce venom to hurt or kill one's prey. Many snakes are venomous.

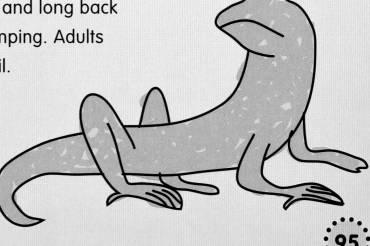

Index

A

adder, 8–9
alligators, 32–33, 34
American alligator, 32
amphibian, definition of, 4, 94
anacondas, 14–15

B

banded sea snake, 28
bearded dragon, 46–47
black mamba, 18–19
blue-tongued skink, 54–55
boa constrictor, 12–13, 24–25
bullfrog, 80–81

C

caimans, 38–39
Chacoan horned frog, 79
chameleons, 42–43
Chinese alligator, 32
cobras, 26–27
common viper, 8–9
constrictors (snakes), 10–15,
  22–25, 94
coral snakes, 20–21
corn snakes, 22–23
crocodiles, 34–35

D

diamondback rattlesnake, 31
diamondback terrapin, 71

E

emerald tree boa, 24–25
European common frog,
  74–75
European common toad,
  84–85

F

fire salamander, 86–87
frilled lizard, 48–49
frogs, 74–83, 85, 94

G

gaboon viper, 16–17
Galapagos tortoise, 64–65
geckos, 40–41
gharial, 36–37
giant treefrog, 77
Gila monster, 56–57
gills, 90, 94
great crested newt, 92–93
green tree python, 11
green turtle, 66

H

habitats, 7, 94
helmeted terrapin, 70
hibernation, 60, 73, 94
horned frogs, 78–79

I

iguanas, 44–45
Indian cobra, 27

J

Japanese giant salamander,
  88–89

K

komodo dragon, 58–59

L

larvae, 4, 94
lizards, 40–61, 62, 94
lungs, 4, 88, 90

M

marine iguana, 44
mudpuppy, 90–91

N

newts, 92–93, 94
North American bullfrog,
  80–81

P

painted turtle, 72–73
poison, 20, 82, 83, 86.
  See also venom
poison dart frogs, 82–83
pythons, 10–11

R

rattlesnakes, 30–31
red-eyed treefrog, 76
reptile, definition of, 4, 95
reticulated python, 10

S

salamanders, 86–93, 95
saltwater crocodile, 34
sea snakes, 28–29
sea turtles, 66–67
skinks, 54–55
slowworms, 60–61
snakes, 4, 8–31, 60, 95
snapping turtle, 68–69

T

tadpoles, 4, 74, 82
terrapins, 70–71, 95
territory, 47, 81, 95
Thai water dragon, 52–53
thorny devil, 50–51
toads, 80, 84–85, 95
tokay, 40
tortoises, 64–65, 95
treefrogs, 76–77
tuatara, 62–63
turtles, 64, 65, 66–73, 95

V

venom, 95
  in lizards, 56
  in snakes, 8, 16, 18, 21,
    26, 30
vipers, 8–9, 16–17

W

white's treefrog, 77

LIFE IN THE
PLAINS

Written by **Catherine Bradley**

PRINCETON ■ LONDON

Published in the United States and Canada by
Two-Can Publishing LLC
234 Nassau Street
Princeton, NJ 08542

www.two-canpublishing.com

© 2000 Two-Can Publishing

For information on Two-Can books and multimedia,
call 1-609-921-6700, fax 1-609-921-3349, or visit our web site at
http://www.two-canpublishing.com

'Two-Can' is a trademark of Two-Can Publishing.
Two-Can Publishing is a division of Zenith Entertainment plc,
43-45 Dorset Street, London W1H 4AB

hc ISBN 1-58728-5568
sc ISBN 1-58728-5711

hc 1 2 3 4 5 6 7 8 9 10 02 01 00
sc 1 2 3 4 5 6 7 8 9 10 02 01 00

Printed in Hong Kong

Photographic credits:
p.4-5 ZEFA/K. Bonath p.7 (top) Bruce Coleman/Andy Purcell (bottom) Bruce Coleman/Michael Freeman p.8 (top right and bottom left) Bruce Coleman/Gerald Cubitt p.9 Bruce Coleman/Peter Ward p.10 Bruce Coleman/Jane Burton p.11 Survival Anglia/J.B. Davidson p.12 (top right) Survival Anglia/Cindy Buxton (bottom left) Survival Anglia/ Jen & Des Bartlett p.13 (top right) Ardea, London/Clem Haagner (bottom) ZEFA/Horus p.14 Bruce Coleman/Hans Reinhard p.15 (top right) Bruce Coleman/Norman Myers (bottom) Bruce Coleman/Gunter Ziesler p.16 Bruce Coleman/Dr Eckart Pott p.17 Planet Earth/Jonathon Scott p.18 Bruce Coleman/L.C. Marigo p.19 ZEFA/Leidman p.20 Hutchison Library/Dr Nigel Smith p.21 (top right) Bruce Coleman/Mark N. Boulton (bottom) Bruce Coleman/D. Houston p.22 Survival Anglia/Richard & Julia Kemp p.23 Bruce Coleman/Simon Trevor

Front cover: Bruce Coleman/R.I.M. Campbell Back cover: NHPA/Peter Johnson

Illustrations by Michaela Stewart. Story by Claire Watts. Edited by Monica Byles.

CONTENTS

Looking at the plains   4
Where in the world?   6
Plants on the plains   8
Animal life   10
Birds in the bush   12
Hunters of the plains   14
Crossing the plains   16
Plains peoples   18
Plain destruction   20
Save the plains   22
Red Leaf and the Great Buffalo Bull   24
True or false?   29
Glossary   30
Index   32

All words marked in **bold** can be found in the glossary.

LOOKING AT THE PLAINS

Most of the world's plains are flat grasslands, with only a few trees to break up the landscape. Most of them stretch, like a shimmering ocean, as far as the eye can see.

In the cooler parts of the world, people have farmed the plains since early times. The rich **soil** provides most of the world's food harvests. Today, the plains are often broken up by fences that mark out different fields. Plains are used to grow crops like wheat, oats, and barley, or to provide food for raising grazing animals, such as cattle and sheep.

The grasslands of Africa are home to a variety of wildlife. Many species feast on the grasses, and are hunted by **predators**. Lions, elephants, and zebras are hunted by people. People have also turned much of the animals' territory into farmland. These wild animals are now confined to the few remaining areas of unspoiled plains.

▼ Trees on the **tropical** plains have thick bark to protect them against fires, and deep roots to tap underground water. Many have spikes to defend their leaves against grazing animals.

WHERE IN THE WORLD?

Most plains lie towards the center of the Earth's continents. Often they are located on the inner side of high mountain ranges, and so are cut off from the sea winds that bring rain. The lack of rain means that there are no great forests on the Earth's plains, because most trees need a lot of water to grow.

The tropical plains lie in belts of hot land on either side of the **Equator**. They do not have seasons such as summer and winter. Instead, they have dry and wet periods.

Temperate grasslands lie further away from the Equator, and are hot or cold depending on the seasons.

Different countries have different names for their plains. In Russia, the plains are called **steppes**. In North America, the grasslands are called **prairies**, meaning meadows. The plains of South Africa are called **veld**, which is Dutch for field. In Africa and Australia, the grasslands are known as **savannahs**. The people of South America call their plains the **pampas** and the **campo**.

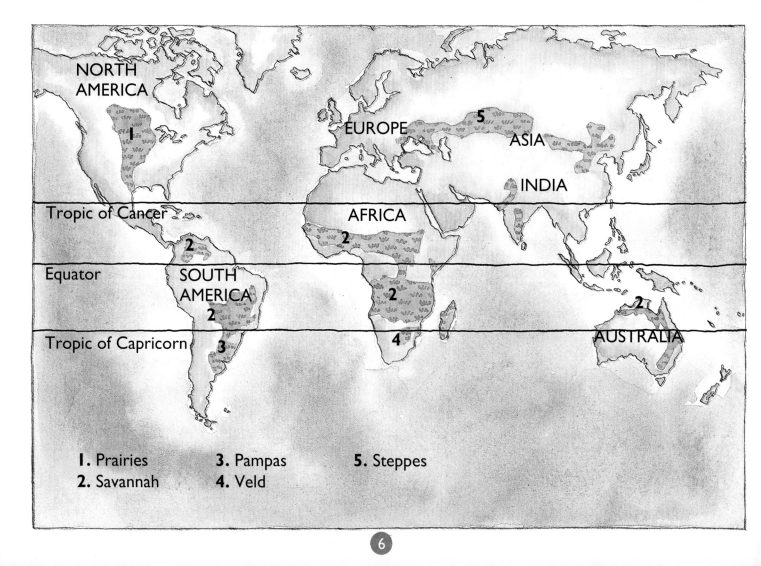

1. Prairies   3. Pampas   5. Steppes
2. Savannah   4. Veld

◀ A combine harvester works its way through a field of ripe wheat in England. The blades cut, or reap, the stalks, then they shake, or thresh, the ears to release the valuable grains.

▼ In Southeast Asia many of the plains are flooded to grow rice, the main food eaten by about half the people in the world. Most of the back-breaking work is still done by hand. This woman from Java is transplanting rice.

PLANTS ON THE PLAINS

Grasses dominate the world's plains. There are about 8,000 species in all, covering about one-quarter of the Earth's surface. They grow well on the open plains because they need a great deal of light. they can survive drought, being trampled, very hot sunlight, fire, and frost. If there is not enough water or heat, they just stop growing until conditions improve. Antarctica is the only area in the world where grasses cannot thrive.

In cooler regions, the grasses tend to remain short. In the tropical grass-lands, however, they can grow to enormous heights.

Among the grasses may grow plants such as dandelions, daisies and clover. Plants that grow from bulbs, such as lilies, also thrive on the plains.

▲ The plains grasses have many uses. In South Africa, a Cape weaver bird perches above its nest. The male has carefully woven the bell-shaped nest from dried grasses to attract a female. The female will approve the nest, then prepare an inside lining to cushion the eggs.

◀ A swollen baobab tree rises from a sisal plantation in Madagascar. The spongy trunk stores rainwater, then shrinks in dry weather. In a drought, elephants have been known to tear off branches to reach the water hidden inside.

► A tumbleweed rolls around a dusty plain in Mexico. These plants develop rounded tops, then wither and break away from the ground during fall. The large, light plant then rolls around the plains, tossed about by the winds. As the weed tumbles, it scatters its seeds over a wide area. Tumbleweeds are considered a nuisance by farmers because they often pile up against fences and fill up small valleys.

FOOD FACTS

● Grass seeds are lightweight and easily carried by the wind. They soon colonize a patch of bare ground, sending out a network of underground stems, which sprout new leaves. Farmers have learned to breed certain varieties to provide plentiful and cheap food crops.

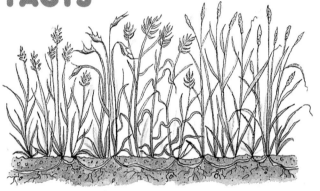

● Some grasses are used to feed farm animals. The farmer may sow a mixture of two or three kinds of grass seed together with clover. In summer, the grass may be cut to make food that will be stored to feed the animals in the winter.

● **Cereals** are grasses that provide food for people. Varieties include oats, maize, wheat, barley, millet, and rice. Popcorn, cornflakes, and corn oil are made from corn. Wheat grains are ground into flour for bread and pasta. Oatmeal is made from oats.

ANIMAL LIFE

In the wild, the plains grasses feed huge herds of **grazers**. Most grazers are **herbivores**. A great variety lives in Africa, including antelopes, giraffes, rhinoceroses, elephants, and zebras. Many of these animals prefer to browse on the trees and bushes. Giraffes feed on the lower branches of the acacia, so these thorny trees end up looking like umbrellas.

Grass leaves and seeds also feed hordes of insects, such as butterflies, and grasshoppers. The soil below is tunnelled and heaped up by termites, or ants. One huge African anthill even had a village built on it!

The south American pampas is home to small grazers such as the mara and cavies, wild relations of the guinea pig. Larger animals, such as kangaroos and wallabies, feed on the savannahs of Australia.

▲ A dung beetle tests a rabbit pellet. These beetles often roll the droppings of elephants and other large animals into smaller balls, then bury them. They lay their eggs in the dung, which provides food for their larvae.

▶ On many of the world's plains, the main protection from predators is to run fast. Some animals live in herds, like these African zebra drinking at a waterhole, so that there are plenty of eyes and ears to spot danger. A lion could be lurking behind any nearby bush.

ANIMAL ANTICS

The South American anteater has a specially shaped snout for digging up ants, termites, and grubs from the soil. It has a long whip-like tongue, which it uses to catch the insects.

Prairie dogs, or marmots, live in North America. They burrow tunnels to house their big communities, or 'towns'. One town was thought to have held up to 400 million prairie dogs.

BIRDS IN THE BUSH

Birds of many different shapes and sizes live on the plains. Clouds of small birds feast on the plentiful seeds and vast numbers of insects.

The African savannah is ruled by the meat-eating vultures. They circle above the plains in search of dead flesh. Marabou storks and ravens also join in the **scavenging**. Eagles and hawks also hunt prey on the plains.

Several flightless birds, such as the South American rhea and the Australian emu, roam the grasslands. These birds are fast runners and tend to be large. The African ostrich can grow to nearly 8 feet (2.4 m) tall. The birds live in flocks and feed on seeds, plants, and even small animals.

▲ Cattle egrets live in Africa near antelope, cattle, and elephants. They perch on an animal's back to eat insects, such as lice or ticks, living there. Egrets warn their hosts of any danger by flying off suddenly.

◀ Two ostriches look after their young. At one month old, the babies can run as fast as an adult – up to 40 miles (64 km) per hour. The ostrich can live up to 70 years and is the world's largest living bird. It has good eyesight to spot its enemies and can kick an attacker to death using the sharp nails on the two toes on each foot.

▶ An African secretary bird stamps on a grasshopper. It eats insects, frogs, lizards, small tortoises, and snakes. Sometimes it flies high, drops its prey, then lands and eats it.

▼ Huge flocks of small birds, such as these pink cockatoos from Australia, swoop over the grassy plains. The cockatoos feed mainly on a variety of insects, fruit, nuts, and grass seeds.

HUNTERS OF THE PLAINS

The best-known African plains dwellers are the hunter cats, such as lions. Lions live in groups, or prides, of up to 30 animals in a territory. They eat mainly wildebeest, zebras, and gazelles. Other African hunters include cheetahs, leopards, hyenas, and jackals.

On the Russian steppes and the prairies of North America the grey wolf was once a mighty hunter. It is now very rare, having been nearly wiped out because of its threat to farm animals and people. In North America, the coyote is now the main predator.

The main hunter on the pampas of South America is the cunning jaguar. It will lie in ambush and stalk for long periods to catch its prey.

SNAKE CHARMER

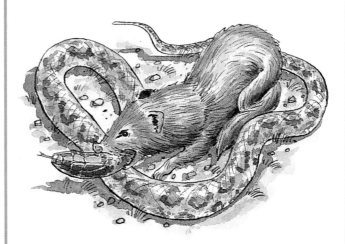

The mongoose is a slim animal, similar to a ferret. Some species are famous for killing snakes. The mongoose has sharp eyesight and can usually dodge a snake's fangs. It also eats insects, rats, snails, worms, and lizards. Some will smash eggs and eat them, too.

◄ The flecked coat of a cheetah **camouflages** it against the sun-dappled grasses. Cheetahs are the fastest short-distance runners of all land animals. They can sprint at 68 miles (110 km) per hour. They hunt mainly during the day for antelopes and gazelles.

Cheetahs are now rare, because many of their old hunting grounds have been turned into farmland. They have also been hunted for their **pelts**. Most cheetahs live in Africa.

► **Carrion** is left by an animal once it has eaten its fill. The scavengers then gather to share the spoils. Here, spotted hyenas and vultures pick a skeleton clean on an African plain. In the background, a solitary marabou stork waits patiently for its turn at the feast.

Scavenging birds often have featherless, bare skin on their necks and heads to help them feed more easily inside the dead animal's body.

▼ A zebra runs for its life, fleeing from a lioness. Often several lionesses will surround their prey so that it cannot escape. When it is killed, the male lions and cubs come to share the meal. Lions have few enemies, and sleep up to 20 hours a day.

CROSSING THE PLAINS

Many of the grazing herds of the plains travel enormous distances in search of food. The wildebeest of the East African plains **migrate** every year in search of fresh feeding grounds in the river valleys. At the beginning of the dry season, the separate herds gather to start the long trek. They are often joined by groups of gazelles and zebras. The immense herds will travel up to 125 miles (200 km) and will often mate on the way. When the rainy season begins, they return to the open plains, where their calves will be born.

Saiga antelopes on the vast Russian steppes also ramble over very long distances in search of fresh food and water. They are known to travel up to 220 miles (350 km) across the steppes in a single year.

DID YOU KNOW?

● Sometimes a plague of locusts comes to the African plains. These insects ride on the wind in huge swarms of up to 50 million. A swarm can rapidly eat enough to feed 400 thousand people for a year.

▶ The best-known migration on the East African plains is that of the wildebeest. They travel in enormous groups of up to 1,000 animals. The lengthy journey is often very dangerous, especially when crossing a rushing river. Many animals do not survive.

▼ On the North American prairies, the bison used to migrate each year, but they are now confined to **national parks**.

PLAINS PEOPLES

The first people are thought to have lived on the plains around 40,000 years ago. They hunted animals and ate berries and roots. Gradually, the people learned to tame some animals and to harvest food crops from some of the plants. Soon, they developed ways of breeding plants and animals to create new ones from wild varieties.

Today, food crops for humans and animals are grown in vast fields all over the world. A range of different animals are kept on the pastures for their meat, milk, or skins.

In many lands, some people live on the plains as **nomads**. They usually keep herds of animals and move from place to place in search of grazing land. On the steppes of Asia, for example, the Mongols and Kazakhs keep herds of cattle, sheep and horses. The animals provide them with food, clothing, and the materials to make tents.

▼ Wealthy farmers use cowboys to ranch cattle on the Mato Grosso plain of South America. The cowboys work on horseback and wear tough leather clothes to protect them from thorns as they ride across the plain.

▶ A young Masai warrior practices a traditional dance. The Masai live on the borders of Kenya and Tanzania in East Africa. They build villages near a water supply and move on when the grass of the surrounding land has been eaten by their cattle. They mainly feed on cow's blood mixed with milk, with a few vegetables, traded from other tribes for meat and skins.

PEOPLE FACTS

● Some of the Aboriginal people of Australia still live by hunting animals and eating wild plants. Most now live in nature **preserves**. In the past, Aborigines would remember long-distance routes across country by learning complex songs which mentioned important landmarks.

PLAIN DESTRUCTION

People have greatly changed the world's plains. Long ago in the northern **hemisphere**, people cleared forests and plowed up the grasses to make farmland. In Britain, 80 percent of the forests were cut down. The wild plants and animals were replaced with domestic crops and herds.

Modern farmers use chemicals, such as fertilizers and pesticides, to help their crops grow better. Some of these chemicals have ruined the soil and even damaged water supplies. Overfarming also leads to **erosion**, when soil is blown or washed away.

On the tropical plains, people have also used the best land for farming. Some farmers have allowed herds to overgraze the grass, again causing erosion. The grass roots hold soil in place, but with grass and soil gone, only bare rock remains and the hungry animals will move on.

DID YOU KNOW?

● Millions of bison used to roam the North American prairies. Overhunted, they now survive only in nature preserves.

● Small burrowing prairie dogs, which were once common, are now scarce.

● Saiga antelope once covered the Russian steppes. Few survive today.

▲ A man proudly displays the hide of a jaguar. These rare animals are hunted for their high-quality fur, which is made into clothes, bags and shoes. Other plains animals that have been hunted close to **extinction** just to provide luxury products, include the rhinoceros, the lion, and the elephant. Many countries around the world now ban the import of any goods made from endangered animals.

▶ Bare soil shows through in Masai country, Kenya. Here, the herds of sheep and goats have been allowed to overgraze. Where the grass has gone, soil quickly blows away. In hot countries such as Kenya, the ruined plains may soon turn into desert.

▼ Fires occur naturally on the African plains in the hot, dry season. Local trees have thick bark to protect them from the heat. The charred grasses soon grow back from the roots. Some fires harm animals and destroy crops.

SAVE THE PLAINS

Of all the people in the world, farmers can help most to save the plains. They can try to use chemical fertilizers more carefully so that the soil is not damaged. They can plant trees and hedges to prevent soil erosion from the wind. If any land has been overgrazed, they can fence it off to prevent animals from damaging it even further.

Farmland on plains at the edge of deserts should be **irrigated** to make the best use of water supplies. Crops that are specially adapted to the dry conditions should be grown. Every few years, farmers should leave parts of their land unfarmed so that the soil can recover its richness.

The wild animals of the plains also need protection. In Africa, many elephants have been killed for their **ivory** tusks, while the spotted cats are gunned down by **poachers** for their pelts. Most of the countries where the African elephant lives keep these animals in national parks and set up armed patrols to protect them. People should refuse to buy products made from ivory and animal fur to stop the trade.

▼ Giraffes must watch out for predators. They sleep for only about 20 minutes each night, divided into three or four short naps. Another greater threat today comes from humans who kill giraffes for their skins and turn their grassland homes into farms.

▼ Large areas of Africa have been set aside for wild animals to live in peace. However, the rhinoceros is still hunted secretly by poachers. There are not very many of these animals left on the plains of Africa today. Rhinos graze on grass, twigs and leaves. White egrets eat the insects that live on rhinos, as well as those turned up in the soil as the rhinos walk along.

PLAIN PERSUASION

Support campaigns

There are many groups trying to stop the killing of plains wildlife. They need money and support to continue. Watch for news on television, the radio, the internet, newspapers, and magazines for how you can help.

Stop the trade

Explain to people why you would not wear fur clothes, or buy products made from rare species.

RED LEAF AND THE GREAT BUFFALO BULL

For thousands of years, people have told stories about the world around them. Often, these stories try to explain something that people do not understand, such as how the world began. This story, told by the Cheyenne of North America, tries to explain how the group of stars we know as the Pleiades came to be.

Long ago, a girl named Red Leaf lived in a teepee on the plains with her seven adopted brothers. Every day, six of the brothers would go out hunting, while the youngest, who was known as Little Brother, would stay behind to chop wood and fetch water. Red Leaf cooked the meat that the brothers brought home, and made and mended their moccasins and clothes. They all took care of each other and were very happy.

One day, six of the brothers went hunting, and Little Brother went to fetch water, leaving Red Leaf alone in the camp. On Little Brother's return, he found Red Leaf gone, and there were signs of a struggle. from the hoofprints, Little Brother knew that the Great Buffalo Bull, who ruled over all the buffalo, had stolen Red Leaf.

When his brothers returned, Little Brother told them his story. All the brothers were afraid of the Great Buffalo Bull, but they knew they must save their precious sister.

The seven brothers built a series of four strong corrals, one inside the other, so that they would have a safe place to run to if they managed to bring back Red Leaf. Little Brother went out and collected anthills in his cloak. He sprinkled them in a steady line, all along the ground inside of the innermost corral.

Then, taking up their very special magic medicine sacks, the seven brothers bravely set off, following the dusty trail of the Great Buffalo Bull's enormous hoofprints.

They travelled for a long time. At last, they came to a hill overlooking the vast plain. Below them, covering the plain as far as they could see, stretched the buffalo herd. Right in the middle was a wide open space, where the Great Buffalo Bull stood, with poor Red Leaf lying nearby.

"We must get a message to Red Leaf, to tell her we are here, " said the oldest brother. He brought out his magic medicine sack, which was made from the skin of a blackbird. As he held it in his hand, it turned into a living blackbird and flew off into the center of the herd, right to the place where Red Leaf lay.

But before the blackbird could deliver the message, it heard the Great Buffalo Bull bellow furiously: "Get away, spy!"

The earth shook, as the Great Buffalo Bull pawed the ground, and the blackbird flew off in fear.

The second brother took out his coyote skin medicine sack. As he held it, it turned into a living coyote, which set off boldly through the buffalo herd until it managed to reach the very place where little Red Leaf lay.

"Get away, spy!" roared the Great Buffalo Bull in a terrible fury, and the cowardly coyote swiftly turned and ran away.

The third brother's medicine sack was made from the skin of a little yellow bird. The bird was so tiny that it reached Red Leaf without the Great Buffalo Bull noticing.

"Red Leaf," whispered the bird, in its tiny voice. "Pull your cloak over your head and wait for your seven brothers to rescue you."

When the little yellow bird returned, Little Brother took out his gopher skin medicine sack. As he placed the skin on the ground, it turned into a living gopher and began to dig right under the herd. Little Brother followed the gopher along its tunnel and came up under Red Leaf's cloak. He led her down the tunnel, leaving her cloak over the hole. Then Red Leaf and her brothers ran as fast as they could to the corrals.

It was not long before the Great Buffalo Bull noticed something was amiss. He pushed Red Leaf's cloak aside with his hoof and discovered the secret tunnel below. Bellowing furiously, he charged off at once in the direction of the brothers' camp, with the rest of the herd hard on his heels. In no time at all, the Great Buffalo Bull was standing outside the corral with his whole herd gathered around him.

"Give me back my Red Leaf!" roared the Great Buffalo Bull.

Inside the corral, the brothers and their sister trembled with fear.

The Great Buffalo Bull began to charge the first corral. Soon, the logs lay scattered at his feet.

"Give me back my Red Leaf," he bellowed again.

"Let me go to him and the rest of you will be spared," brave Red Leaf begged her brothers.

But Little Brother insisted that they would all be safe and sound.

It was not long before the Great Buffalo Bull had tossed aside the logs of the next three corrals. But when he came to the line of anthills, he found that every grain of sand had turned into a huge rock. The whole herd charged at these from every side, until it seemed that they would surely reach Red Leaf and the seven brothers, who quaked inside.

"Have no fear," said Little Brother, as he shot an arrow into the sky. A tree appeared, reaching skywards.

Little Brother helped his sister climb into the branches and the other six brothers followed.

As Little Brother swung himself last into the tree, the Great Buffalo Bull broke through the anthills. He charged at the tree, taking huge chunks out of its trunk. Each piece the bull tore off immediately joined up again, and the tree remained as good as new.

As for Red Leaf and her seven brothers, they kept climbing the tree until they reached the sky. And you can still see them there. Red Leaf is the main star, and Little Brother is the smallest one, over to one side.

TRUE OR FALSE?

Which of these sentences are true and which ones are false?
If you have read this book carefully, you will know the answers.

1. Tropical lands have spring, summer, fall, and winter.

2. A small mongoose can catch and kill a snake.

3. Popcorn, cornflakes, and corn oil are made from barley.

4. Prairie dogs live in a network of tunnels called a town.

5. South American cowboys wear clothes made from woven grasses.

6. There are about one million species of grass in the world.

7. Giraffes will sleep for up to 14 hours every day.

8. The ostrich can live up to 70 years.

9. A swarm of locusts can rapidly devour enough food to feed 400 thousand people for one year.

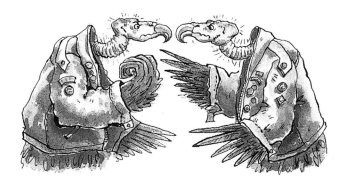

10. Scavenging birds, such as vultures, often have bare skin on their heads.

GLOSSARY

● **Camouflage** hides an animal against its surroundings to protect it from predators, and can help it to capture prey.

● The **campo** is the tropical grassland in South America.

● **Carrion** is dead flesh.

● **Cereals** are grasses that have been developed by people to provide food.

● The **Equator** is the imaginary line round the Earth, halfway between the North and the South Poles.

● **Erosion** is the wearing away of soil or rock by wind, rain and floods, ice or frost.

● **Extinction** occurs when the last of an animal or plant species dies out. This often happens when animals are overhunted by people or other species, or when they lose their food or feeding place.

● **Grazers** are animals that feed on grasses or other plants.

● A **hemisphere** is one half of the Earth. There are two halves: the northern and the southern hemispheres.

● **Herbivores** eat only grass and other plants. They have special teeth with ridged surfaces to grind the grass into small pieces.

● To **irrigate** is to artificially water land that naturally tends to be dry. Water is often channelled through ditches.

● **Ivory** is what the tusks of elephants, and some other animals, are made from. It was once used to make piano keys.

● To **migrate** means to move from one area to another. This often takes place once a year as the seasons change and animals and birds look for fresh supplies of food and a warmer climate.

● **National parks** are large areas of land protected by law, where the landscape cannot be changed and the birds and animals cannot be harmed by hunters or collectors.

● **Nomads** are people who move from place to place following animal herds, which provide them with food and materials to make clothes and tents.

● **Pampas** are the temperate grasslands of south America. Pampa is the Spanish word for plain.

● **Pelts** are the skins or furs of animals.

● **Poachers** are people who kill animals illegally to make money from selling their meat, skins, horns, tusks, or other parts.

● **Prairies** are the temperate grasslands of North America.

● **Predators** are animals that hunt and kill other animals.

● **Preserves** are a special areas set aside under the laws of a country for certain people or animals to live in.

● **Savannahs** are the tropical grasslands in Africa, South America, and Australia.

● **Scavenging** is when animals or birds feed on the remains of animals that they have not hunted for **themselves.**

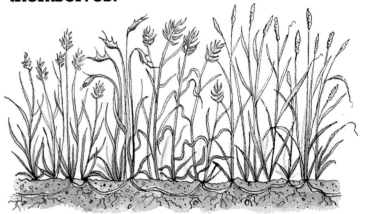

● **Soil** is the top layer of ground in which plants grow. It is made up of ground-down particles of rock.

● The **steppes** are the temperate grasslands of both southeast Europe and Asia.

● **Temperate** describes the mild climate that is found in lands on either side of the tropical area.

● **Tropical** describes the hot climate around the Equator.

● **Veld** is the temperate grassland of South Africa.

INDEX

Africa 4, 6, 10, 12, 13, 14, 15, 16, 19, 22
Asia 6, 7, 18
Australia 6, 10, 12, 13, 19

birds 8, 12, 13, 15, 23
Britain 20

campo 6
crops 4, 7, 9, 20, 21, 22

erosion 20, 22
Europe 6

farming 4, 7, 18, 20, 22
fertilizer 20, 22

grass 4, 6, 8, 9, 20, 21
grazing animals 4, 10, 16, 20

herbivores 10

India 6
insects 10, 12, 13, 14, 16, 23
irrigation 22
ivory 22

Kenya 19, 21

Madagascar 8
Mexico 9
migration 16

national parks 16, 22
nomads 18, 19
North America 6, 10, 14, 16, 20

overgrazing 20, 21, 22

pampas 6, 10, 14
plains people 18
plants 8, 9
poachers 22
prairie 6, 10, 16, 20
predators 4, 10, 12, 14, 15, 21

Russia 6, 14, 16, 20

savannah 6, 10, 12
scavengers 12, 15
South Africa 6, 8
South America 6, 10, 12, 14, 18
steppe 6, 14, 16, 18, 20

trees 4, 6, 8, 10, 21, 22

veld 6